EVEN MY FINGERTIPS REMEMBER YOU

MANYA CHHABRA

FanatiXx® Publication

Rourkela | Mumbai | Delhi NCR | Ahmedabad

Even My Fingertips Remember You
By Manya Chhabra

ISBN: 978-93-7406-954-7 (Paperback)
ISBN: 978-93-7406-743-7 (E-book)

First Edition – 2026

This is an Original Work of the Author.
All works of the author's imagination.
Any resemblance to actual persons, living or dead, is purely coincidental.

For permissions, inquiries, or feedback:
Email: outreach@fanatixx.info
Instagram: @fanatixxpublication

ABOUT THE POET

I'm Manya and, I absolutely adore life. I have been writing ever since, I was 10 years old and embarrassingly enough my first poetry was about being a princess and eating chocolates.

Fair to say, I've come a long way. This book is a piece of my heart and, I hope you enjoy reading it as much as, I did writing it.

I wrote this when, I was 18. Well, I'm 21 now and, I finally have mustered up the courage to put it out. This book consists of 50 poetries. It's a collection, following the storyline of having it all and then losing it. There's love, heartbreak, grief, reflection- everything in there. When, I first started it, I wanted to follow the stages of grief in order but to have felt it myself, I realized that there is no order.

Grief is a table, I sit and take my morning and evening tea.

+2 surprise poetries that, I wrote for my mum and dad.

I wouldn't be here without you, Thank you.

I’m writing to let you go-

I yearn for you,
a love that hasn't met me yet,
the hands, I'm yet to hold,
the arms that won't let go of me,
someone who'll put me above all.
I wait for you,
linger uncomfortably at your door.
In my sleep, I dream of you,
when awake, I write you poems.
We haven't met yet,
but in my head, you stand at my door.
You're making me pasta
while, I sit on the shelf-
I look at you, I adore.
In my head, we already made it,
I pick the children up from school,
you continue to make me pasta
but this time, for two.

We were two strangers
sitting on a bus,
love watched from the corner
and to himself, he laughed.
I believed, I was too hard to love
and to you, loving me was like breathing.
I never thought, I'd find it,
in my head, I was always reeling.
A loving partner, a peace driven home,
uncontrollable laughter, dancing to our favorite song,
reading books together, making iced vanilla latte,
watching the same tv show over and over again,
breakfast in bed on a random Friday,
you'd bring me flowers just because,
I'd click a thousand pictures
you'd keep one in your wallet
and one in your work register.

I'd surprise you with home cooked meals,
probably write a book about you,
I'm a little slow at falling
but when, I do
I'm all about these grand gestures.
I'd leave you notes on the mirror
and one in your lunchbox,
'I'm proud of you handsome'
that's how, I'd start.
I'd remember your words,
put 'marrying you' on my vision board,
I said, I'm slow at falling
but in measures of love,
I never fall short.

He tells me it's okay, I'm right here,
right where you want me to be
my heart takes a breath,
still fighting my brain, 'cos how could it be?
no one stays after this, nobody dares
once they see how hard it is to love me
they tend to always leave,
so why is he standing here
and saying all the right things,
my brain usually answers the question
before the question leaves my lips,
it's crazy how it matched,
he even used the same *font*
but how could it be,

this love was reserved for the books-
so, I've been told,
way too many times,
at moments where it felt wrong.
I had just accepted my fate
so why? how is he standing at my door,
how is he holding my hand
and not hurting what once, I repaired.
I'm still frightened to let him in
so, I pull away,
a gentle, 'I'm afraid, I can't'
he says, "it's alright, I understand, I'll wait".
God how could it be,
I was so sure, I lost.
Everyone will find their someone someday
but, I thought that,
I didn't stand a chance.

I have seen hate change people
but in you, I saw love do the part,
You say, "you don't like yourself"
and suddenly our thoughts are polar apart.
You bring me noodles packed up in box
and say, "have it before you go for your early morning job".
You see, I'm not a morning person
and cooking early does sound like a job
and so, I thank you but God, you really make it hard,
hard to keep my distance to,
you make me want to forget,
how he couldn't say goodbye
when, he left
and no, I'm not over it,
I still walk through a road covered in broken glass
but God the amount, I'd bleed
if it meant for you to be my fresh start.

You see, I'm a hopeless romantic,
I picture the ending before the movie starts
and with you, I believe it to be happy,
I could be betting on the stars.
We would have a little house,
white picket fence,
you'd kiss me goodbye
before you'd go and drop off our children
and here, I'm doing it again
and, I could be so graciously wrong
but you turn me around,
my hand wrapped up in your arm,
you say, "I like you"
and my imaginary house still stands.

The intimacy of being tired together,
my head on your chest.
I feel so heavy lately
but with you, I innately rest.
I've never been so calm,
the weight is off of my chest
and with my shoulders, I sigh
"Have we ever met?"
'cos you feel like a home,
I already belong to before,
before I even moved
to this city, to this shore.
You say, "you look so pretty"
and suddenly pretty isn't just a word anymore,
it is as if a bouquet of flowers
just got delivered to my door.
"I'm very fond of the sea" you say,
I'd go anywhere with you,
I'm very much of a home body
but as you move,

my home moves along with you.
'Are you going to let go?', I keep thinking to myself
but you pull me in tighter
and my heart starts to melt.
I've never believed in love at first sight,
always questioned it with a how and why
but getting to know you
seems like something worth a try.
I ask you if it's getting late
as, I see the sky turn
You pull me in your arms
and say, you're already where you belong
I blush, I sigh-
my anxiety filled nerves.
I've never let someone in
no, not this close.
"You can trust me", you say
as if you already knew,
our fingers intertwined
God, is this really true?

You ask me to stay and, I would stay forever
but, I tell you 'no'
just so you think of me better.
I put on my boots,
you help me close the zipper,
you say, "I'm walking you home"
and suddenly, I'm a love letter.
We talk on the way home,
and, I keep wishing for it to last,
as we reach my doorstep
you tell me, "I really like your laugh"
and there goes my insecurity,
I'm all wrapped up in your arms
still blushing, still wishing as you speak,
"When can, I take you out for a dance?"

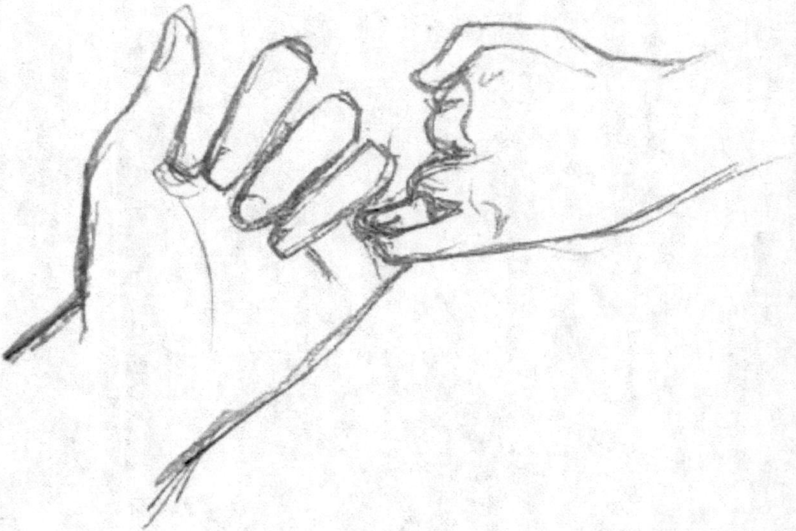

I want to be the gentle breeze on your face
amidst all the rain,
I want to be the one you come home to
in the middle of afternoon,
when you'll say, you got off early
and I'll say, I just woke up
but my morning couldn't have been better
now that, I feel your touch.
You'll tell me how your day went
even if it's just past noon,
'cos even an hour feels like a lifetime without you.
I'll ask you if you're hungry
as I think, 'what's in the fridge?'
just so, I could cook you something
real quick

but you point towards the bag you brought
and say, “I got your favorite doughnuts”.
and I’ll squeak with happiness,
“I couldn’t have loved you more”
and you say, “you will”
as you open the top right drawer
and there it is, another surprise,
another ‘this made me think of you’
another ‘I love you’
wrapped up in a small box,
I’ll say, “you remembered”
as I unbox.
“I saw you staring at them last Wednesday in the store”,
“But it was too expensive”,
“Compared to you, it was no worth”
my tear filled eyes,
as you put them in my ear,
“they look so cute on you”
death is only what, I fear.

I wrap my arms around you
and suddenly there is no pain,
all the years of heartbreak that lead me to you
suddenly seem not so in vain.
I think of ways, I could repay you
make your day somehow
but you pull me in closer
as if you knew what, I think, Wow!
I've prayed lifetimes for this love,
wrote about thousand poetries utmost
but, I never got this close
until, I saw you standing at my balcony
in the middle of night
with your hand holding a sign
"Will you be my girlfriend?"
Yes or No
either ways, I'm yours
to have or to hold.

If you were a soldier,
I'd write letters in your name
I'd tell you each and everything
along with the unnecessary but relevant details.
I'd spare you no sorrows,
I'd take all of your heartache
and when you were done fighting for our country,
I'd make our home, your safe space.
We would've gotten married,
meet on a subway or a train.
If you were a doctor,
our parents would've set us up,
they would've sent us on our first date,
I would've worn my blue dress
along with my sparkly tights,
I would've dressed up a little too extra
compared to you
but to you, it would've felt right.

We would have talked about our fears,
not knowing that losing you would one day
become my biggest
but for the moment,
the thought, 'what if you don't like me' would suffice.
We would've shared a brownie
and you would've saved me the first and the last bite
and somehow, I would've known
that you were it, for the rest of my life.
I'd clap at your every victory
and be with you when everything feels wrong.
I would've stayed with you,
no matter the storm.
If you were a writer,
I'd read all of your books,
build myself a book shelf just to store all of them in.

I'd re-read the chapters,
highlight my favorite parts and even though, I'm not much of a poet,
I would've tried to write you as the light to my darkest parts.
If you were just you,
someone, I raced with in the school yard,
someone who shared his tiffin with me
and made sure to always make me laugh,
I would've loved you the same.
I mean, I already do,
'cos there is not a single lifetime or scenario that exists
where, I don't end up with you.

I'm laying here in your arms,
it's the safest place, I've ever known,
you pull me closer
and it feels as if, I just reached home.
You're the destination, I long to reach
I would travel anywhere for you.
I've never been good at speaking
so, I'm hoping
that you can read.
My tears imprint my face,
if you're gone- who will wipe them for me?
You're the metaphor,
it took me ages to write
so how am I supposed to
just let you leave?

I think you're one person
who was specially curated for me
and no one compares
to the way you make me feel.
You're home to my vacation stricken self
who keeps aimlessly wandering,
you're the fresh cold breeze.
You're sunsets and iced coffee,
you're the feeling of being at home
even when, I'm stuck in an unfamiliar lobby.
I fall for you, like leaves in the autumn
and you're there to catch me,
You're like the moon on the ride home
who seems to follow me blindly.
I love you
and, I could tell you a thousand times.
I love you,
and it still wouldn't amount.

I'd rearrange the alphabets
just so, I could call you my love.
People say love is violent
for you, I'd change the way they thought.
I think to myself
about the ways, I could express my love
but the sun, the sea, the moon-
nothing seems enough.
For you, I'd stay up late
weave your words, as you speak
I'd make the most beautiful sweater
the one, I hope I get to keep.
For you, I'd cross rivers,
think of you on the way back
I thought of getting a souvenir
but nothing seemed to match your laugh.

God knows what, I would do without you,
you're the only home, I've ever known
and whenever you're around,
it feels like, I belong.
You're my comfort look
at every party,
my comfort book
in every library,
with you, I'm never alone
and without you,
I'm never home.
Now it may seem cliche
but you're everything, I've learned about love.
As the poets might say-
You're the lantern
when, I'm stuck in the dark,
you're the hand that, I hold onto
'cos you never let me fall.

People fall in love,
but, I grew in love with you.
for me every day is well spent
as long as, I'm with you.
I may run out of lines
but, I never not adore you,
you're the fairytale, I wished for,
tossing a penny in every pool.
I'm in love with you in sickness and through health,
I'm in love with you every day and with every breathe,
I'm in love with you
and that's all, I have to say
'cos no poems could amount
but you're the reason
that, I stand here today.

Loving you mended me
and for the longest time,
it was the closest thing, I did to loving myself.
I chose you every sunrise, every sunset,
my dreams embodied your laughter,
my heart embraced your pain.
I carried you in my heart for so long
that, I forgot about the void that others had made.
loving you was the closest thing to being human,
loving you was my religion, my prayer.
You were my solace,
my every good deed.
without you, I'm lost,
I'm a cut that always bleeds.
loving you was holy,
loving you was my biggest sin,
I sometimes confuse between loving you
and breathing.

You say, I don't care for you
then why is it
that you occupy my mind the most,
why is it that you are a question
always lingering,
never answered utmost.
You say, I don't care
when, I would grow gardens
just to show my affection,
when, I would write you
the most profound words
just so you could see your own reflection
and yet you say, I couldn't have cared less
but how could it be true
when, I put you above everything else
including myself too.

I'm half in love with you
half of you, I still hold,
half of me can't let you go,
the other half, you never showed.
Half agony, half hope,
I look at you with my eyes closed
You're always around,
I'm tagging along
can you see me?
so in love with you, I sound.
In the crooks of your neck,
I put my hands,
I put down my sorrows,
all the times, I've had to pretend.

I try to behold,

there's something, I sense

you said you don't love me

then why are you making amends?

I worship the floor

you stepped upon,

I'm the stuck in the notes

of your cologne,

you said you don't love me

it doesn't make sense,

you said you don't love me

then why are you at my door again?

Maybe in another lifetime,
I won't spend my time
writing too much about
all things you said and did
that really crossed the line,
I won't have you on my mind
and, I wouldn't wait for your call
I'd be happy,
probably happier than, I was before.
Maybe in another lifetime,
you would've tried to make me stay,
to keep me and not just throw it all away.
Maybe in another lifetime,
you would've loved me back
and, I wouldn't have to spent a lifetime
trying to get over what we had.

'How could you do this to me?'
I'm pacing back and forth,
why can't, I let you go
and just move forward.
You're holding me back
with your claws deep in my head,
how do, I let you go,
win this battle without
your help.
You didn't have to do this
I loved you more than me.
Did you really have to do this-
show me
how cruel you can be.
I cannot believe my own words,
they sound like a made up lie.
I'm here writing notebooks
worth poetries
just 'cos you couldn't say goodbye.

somedays my bed is water

and, I can do nothing but drown in it.

I woke up to this bruising feeling,
that, I can't text you or call,
that you're just a mere memory,
I can't help but recall.
I couldn't get out of bed,
the monsters in my head
seem to have won
and now, we're not only distant,
you're just gone.
I can't tell you how my day went
and ask you about yours,
I can't tell you that, I met a cat
on the way to work,
neither can, I convince you
into getting one for us.

Let's be real, it was never going to work
but God, I really thought that it was,
I wrote a thousand poetries,
put pictures up on my vision board,
I even made itinerary to all the places,
I wanted to go
but there was never a scenario
that you weren't a part of.
I'm scared, I'll never have it,
that you were it for me
and, I just lost.
Someday, you'll be laughing with the love of your life
and, I'll just watch from afar.

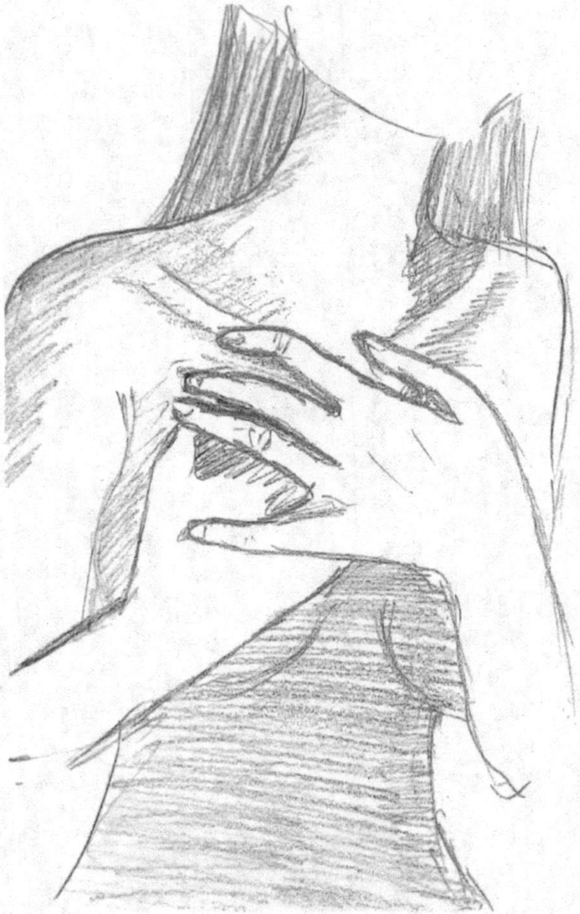

The inevitable melancholy that surrounds
when, I think of you,
actually when, I think of you not being there
for all my happy moments
and all the grief stricken ones,
for all my Monday mornings and my late-night coffee runs.
I miss going swimming with you,
even though we never went,
God, we didn't get to go swimming,
how could we ever end.
I miss you on the sour days
and the days when, I get to see the sun,
but it's all the same,

laughter hiding the misery of me not being the one.
I have a feeling,
it's this scratchy old thought
that just revived when,
I saw you leaving in your car,
I'm not the one,
I'm actually the one before you find it,
exactly what you were looking for
and then there's no denying it.
It's a horrible manifestation to write this,
but if this is really my fate,
I guess, I can't fight it.

I miss you in an unbearable sort of way,
it consumes me,
eats me alive.
In my dream, I hold onto you
with my hands covered in rope burns,
I fear waking up,
I fear my empty hands,
I fear that one day you'll be gone
and with my memories, I'll sit alone
but you're already gone,
aren't you?
I'm just not ready to let it sit,
my heart is burning up in the flames,
while, I sit there pretending, it'll rain.

it'll rain, you'll come back, I know
I know.
It's useless to sit here,
in the middle of your absence and
the memories of your laughter, I get that,
I really do,
but to take a step ahead
is something, I don't think,
I can ever pull myself to do.
I stare at the ceiling, I swear, I still feel you around,
like you're always lingering
and, I'm always longing
for you to one day, come around.

I wake up to this sickening feeling every day,
the inability to text you or call.
I broke down yesterday,
in front of everyone- I yelled,
"You can leave me too
like everybody does."
'For me, my everybody was you'
I went on my usual walk,
came back a little too early,
I couldn't fathom you leaving,
it didn't sit right with me at all.
You changed your profile picture,
It's you but a few years back.
You changed it to the person,
who loved me despite everything

to someone who barely remembers my laugh
or maybe you do,
the thought of you suffering alone got to me yesterday,
it made me sick to my stomach
but then someone reminded me that
you leaving was your own decision.
You must have thought it through right,
pictured me out of your life.
Mom told me to stop stressing,
someday someone will love me right.
A guy walked past me in college few days ago,

He had your build, the way you walked,
he seemed to have perfected it.
I watched from all the way back,
I could've sworn it was you.
my grief started to unpack.
Suddenly, my heart was in two
but he just walked past.
No, he wasn't you
how could anyone be,
but the effect you had on me
about it, I had no clue.
God, you're gone.
Sometimes, I can't put an end to it,
sometimes, I wonder, I'll meet someone
but again,
he won't be you, will it?

Every now and then, I look around.
I’ve been preaching people of happiness
and how it’s found within,
but every now and then, I cry
when, I see nobody standing here.
I’ve been laughing and lying
while, I’m still holding onto your memories,
I keep giving life yet another try.
Every day, I wake up to something
reminding me of you
and every day, I stay a little longer in bed,
more than, I intend to.

You've been long gone,
it just hasn't sit with me yet.
You've been long gone,
no, this can't be it.
I see lovers laughing,
strangers out on their first date,
I see best-friends eating together
and in all of them,
I can't help but see your face.
You're all around, as if you never left.
You're still in here, always
like a secret, well kept.

I keep saying, I want true love
about my wants, I rave,
but whenever love knocks at my door,
I'm too hesitant to cave.
I dream about him opening the car door
but in reality, I never make it to the date
'cos the heartache you gave keeps me occupied
and in solitary, I suffer like a slave.
'His heart would hurt to break mine',
I look for love with faith
but never have, I let someone in
ever since you got up and left me to fate.
You walk all over me,
the blood of my expectations on your feet
I let you walk all over me,
the length of my love for you- it reeks.
Someday someone will want me,
and he will match his actions to his speech.
Someday someone will want me,
I tell myself every night before, I sleep.

When will this hurt turn bittersweet
when will, I get to come home to you
without having a distance to rethink.
I keep longing for a hug
that, I'll never receive
and this distance between us
is increasing my torment
piece by piece,
there are no hands to hold,
no arms that can contain me.
you're one thing, I yearn for
with every prayer, every wish.
I wish, I could hold you close
I yell, I break, I scream.
how long will the torture last,
how long will this keep you from me.

You leave me stranded
with my eyes wide open to see,
you collecting your things
and leaving the baggage right here.
You don't want to take me along
but only if you knew,
I'd travel any corner of this world
if it meant, I'd get to be with you.
You leave me no goodbyes
no lingering hugs,
a stretch of silence growing between us.
I watch you leave
and feel my heart being ripped out
I yell to make you stay
but, I can't hear my own sound.
Only if you knew, I keep feeding myself these lies
'cos you do know everything
but you still won't leave me a goodbye.

Does it mean you'll return
or does it mean you'll forget,
I can't keep myself from falling
like tears on my bed.
I wait for you like a child,
hoping you'll return
it's late and,
I should probably sleep
but my thoughts are on a run.
I wait and wait and wait,
will you ever return
or was the silence that you gave me
a goodbye, I couldn't comprehend.

I collect your words

and bead them in a string around my neck,

sometimes they make me feel so pretty

and others,

they choke me death.

Maybe if, I called you at night
cried while I screamed at you,
asked you for reasons
the answer to all the why(s),
then probably you'd see
the damage that loving you and losing you
did to me.
It's hard to be friends
when we were always a little more
but letting you go is harder
so, I think I'll just suffer alone.
I'm not trying to victimize myself
but what you did was pretty wrong
and the worst part is
I'd let you do it again

and that is why,
I had to put an end.
You lost me that day
and probably, I lost a bit of myself too
‘cos lately, I have been acting
a little stranger for me to be familiar to.
I haven’t written or slept,
the nightmares you left me with
push me closer to the edge.
I’ve been running away, avoiding
the footnotes of your breathe,
only to come home to your
'You moved on so easily and never loved me enough' text.

I'll write until my fingertips can touch yours again.

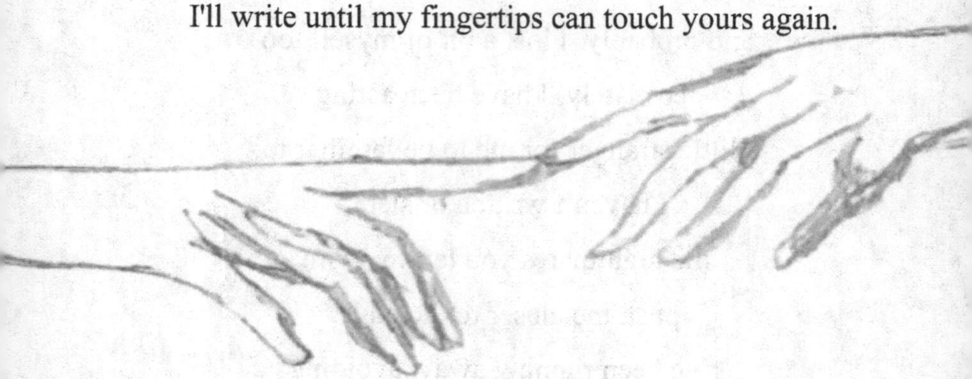

I stare at the empty paper,
with our memories in my hand
waiting, like any minute now
our love would pour through my hands.
I keep on reminiscing you and all the dates that we went on.
I remember your favorite coffee and your favorite spot to sit.
I remember it like the back of my hand,
how you held my hand while you drove,
how, I sang to you screaming in your ears
as if it was a live show.
I miss you,
I made you my home
and God when, I tell you
I've never felt this homesick before.

I want someone nice, I say
but you don’t hear it, I guess
‘cos all my life, I keep asking,
I cut around my corners, I keep bending myself
to fit the idea of being someone easy,
someone who has no shortcomings,
someone who is always calm,
unwillingly so-
who keeps quite and agrees with everything
and puts up with your ability to
never show.
She’s easy to love,
far easier than me,
she never dreads the future,
I don’t think she cares about it really.
She lives in the present, a day at a time
and all your past mistakes are forgiven,
barely remembered by.
She waits,
her patience could hold storms,
‘you didn’t show up’,
it’s fine, another day, I guess.
She barely sees it,

your uninterested eyes,
your casualness,
when it comes to being there for her after fights,
your absent calculations for when she gets off work,
your inability to be concederate.
You might think she's blinded
and rightfully so-
love has that effect
but isn't it two way street though?
I don't think she's blinded,
I think she's just true
to all the promises, you couldn't keep-
she- ah, I hold them against you.
'cos it isn't your inability at times,
it's your ignorance and oblivious perception of yourself,
who believes you to be the man of my dreams,
simply as a man who makes no efforts.

Sometimes I
think about the very first day you left me
and how hard it was,
like every cell in my body just wanted to ring you up,
just wanted to hear your voice,
the voice that had been ringing in my ears ever since, I saw you
the laugh, your smile that never left my mind.
and my everlasting love for you,
even when you were never mine.
It was slowly killing me
to be here without you
but also preparing me
for when you leave.
when this ringing voice is the only thing close enough to you
when our memories
are packed up in suitcases, that you left at home,
when you no longer remember my name
while yours is the only thing that remains.

she is going to fall in love
with the same pair of eyes that I did
and, I'll just watch.
I know, it's not fair to feel this feeling,
it is self-depreciating to say the least.
I want him to be happy
but the thought, 'without me?' stings
I'm not ready to move past it,
‘is he?’
He should though,
staying in the middle does reek.
It's like, I'm battling on the inside,
transitioning between how, I should
and how, I actually feel.
I bet she’s pretty
no, I shouldn’t do that
think of all her strengths
as something, I lack.
I hope she makes him happy
but is it wrong,
if, I don’t have it in me
to watch.

I'm sad and to be honest, tired
I feel everything yet nothing at all,
I feel like a whole new person
who is too different from the me that, I recall.
I haven't cried in weeks
but tears have rolled off of my cheeks
and as crazy as it sounds,
I don't like this strong version of me.
I like me reckless,
crying about little things,
the one who makes mistakes,
the one who isn't really weak.

I like me vulnerable,
caring about every little thing.
the one who over-stresses,
the one who always has a lot to bring.
I like me broken,
a little bit bruised,
the one who carries her memories along,
the one who isn't someone you can use.
I like me the way, I was before
before, I met you
before you took the best parts of me
and decided that, I wasn't for you.

Every time, I asked you to go,
I wanted you to stay.
Every time, I said, “I didn’t want to talk”,
I needed a hug.
Every time, I didn’t smile,
I wanted you to notice.
Every time, I ran away,
I wanted you to run behind.
I wanted you to care,
to acknowledge that, I was upset.
I wanted you to catch me half way through,
and not let me sleep
without a smile on my face.
I wanted you to communicate,
I wanted you to care,

I wanted you to sit in the silence with me
no matter if what you did wasn't fair.
I wanted you to make an effort
to show me that you were sorry,
to show me that my being upset,
had an effect on your glory.
I just wanted to be loved,
and not left alone.
For once, I wanted someone,
whose heart would hurt
to see me torn.

You held your anger
like you should've held me
and, I kept believing
everything, I couldn't see,
how can you say you love me
and still not try,
how can you say you love me
and still make me cry.
I wish that you cared,
I wish that you were here
I keep writing songs about you
that nobody hears.
You're a language,
I'm no longer fluent in
but is the only one, I know
and if my love was water
your tree must have overflowed.

I might see you tomorrow
didn't quite think it would be this hard for me.
I spent the entire week planning
How, I'd wear that little dress
the dress that,
might make you regret
ever hurting me.
Two years ago,
I waited three for you come
and now,
I'm afraid of you
actually showing up.

I'm over you
over your voice or your text
and honestly, that's all the pieces,
I ever had of you,
until you just left.
now we are distant
just like the kilometers between us
and you're a memory, long forgotten
with a scar that still hurts.

I watched you slowly give up on me,
let the hands you held go.
I saw you tolerate my love,
but where did yours go?

I'll let you love me and let others sew
the wounds you leave me with.
I'll let you hurt me,
until there's no part of me left
with no needles in.

Who am I when, I'm not loved?

Sometimes when the music gets low,
my mind turns loud
and even though there is no one around,
it feels as if, I'm being stabbed
and my heart's being cut out.
Now, that's a funny way to tell you
that it gets lonely
and, I don't know who, I am when the curtains close
but it's not the present that, I fear
It's the fear of always being this alone.
what if all my life, I have no hands to hold
no arms that could contain me.
What if all my life, I keep running around
but there's no place that awaits me.

what do you do,
if you're covered in melancholy
and there's nothing
that you can do.
what do you do,
when sadness is that part of you
that makes you, You.
How do you heal,
how do you grow,
how do you hold hands with your pain,
while you're also letting it all go.
How do you tell someone,
how you feel,
when there are storms in your head
but outside, the sky is clear.

how do you breathe,
when there are knots tied up in your chest
and the fear feels real
how do you tell someone,
the density of what you feel.
would they understand,
would the care
when pain is the only language
you can freely translate.
would they listen,
would they dare,
to hold onto me
while I collapse
in thin air.

I sometimes scream at these walls
why do, I feel so caged up,
I've let it go years ago
but why do, I still fear your touch.
How could you be so cruel
yet hide it under a disguise
and how could, I be so naive
when, I let you inside.
I swear, I thought you changed,
I swear, I thought, I was the problem
for you to behave that way
and God was, I wrong
how did, I ended up giving you
the keys
to the house you still haunt.
I look at me with shame,
my hands tainted with my own blood,
you were always the monster
but why when the game of blame begun,
I was both the winner
and the one who lost.

Somedays,
I promise myself, I'll never let you in.
the others,
I realize, you never left to begin with.

When did, I start to envy love?
honestly, I can't recall,
when did, I start wanting it so bad
that, I gave up everything for the cost.
I’ve always had it in me
but, I lost track of my reflection.
When did the word ‘sufficient’,
become such an unattainable achievement.
I’m a lonesome night,
I’m his wasted tears
but who am I,
when, I'm not influenced.

I don't know and that's such an inequitable defeat.
Why am, I fighting this battle
if, I don't share the will to win.
I'm a lost dynasty, a submerged piece of land,
waiting for an errant to reclaim it,
waiting for someone to see,
I'm so much more than what they declare me to be.
I'm the forgotten leaf, the friend left behind,
someone people hand their grief to,
someone who turns it into a rhyme.

I think, I loved you very much
but never got the chance to say.
In these questionable small talks,
I think there's a bit of love that still stays.
You told me, you loved me,
it was right person wrong time.
I'd still open the door-
if someday, you decided to come by.
We don't talk so often
no, not like before
I barely know how your day went,
let alone the stories that you hold.

I still think about you,
sometimes when the sky turns
or when, I'm watching a romantic movie
and my heart starts to ache,
we used to watch them together,
there's barely one that we didn't,
you're still the main character
if my life were a film.
You've been long gone,
there are years between us now
yet, I sometimes wonder,
'do you think about me now?'

I've almost texted you a million times,
in my head, you never leave
all the unsaid, I love you(s)
in my head, I say, I scream.
I'm embracing you in my arms
while you're in a deep sleep,
you actually love me in my head
and there is no reason for you to leave.
In my head, you didn't break my heart,
you actually helped me heal
and, I know it may seem surreal to you
but the version, I had of you in my head
feels just so real.

In my head, you're still my hero,
you're my savior -
the reason, I breathe.
In my head, you didn't leave me stranded
In my head, you wiped my tears.
In my head, I still love you
at least we have that one thing,
we don't argue on,
there's one common ground
that you concede.
Now, the version of you in my head may be
the love of my life
but there's a reason he lives in my head
and not where you reside.

I sometimes forget the damage loving you brought to me,
the way, I can never love anyone the same,
the way, I'll always look for you in them
and wish for it to not end the same.
I tend to forget the damage you brought to me,
the bits and pieces of you
that never left.
I tend to forget how much, I love you
and on one of these nights,
I remember it again.

I’ve been hoarding your words,
how can, I love you better?
how could you let me go?
I keep writing this, 'I’ll never send you' letter.
I’m still waiting on your call,
the plant in my garden grew,
I water it daily and so, I wait for you.
You know, I never said how much, I hated it-
the silence you gave me
for reasons, I never understood.
I made a new friend,
he drives and, I sit by
and on every traffic light,
I tragically wait to see you pass by.
I’ve been dreaming a lot
the size of my heart grew
and now it holds
even more of you.

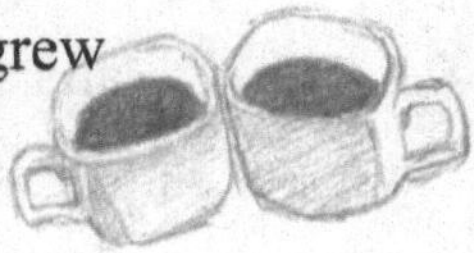

The word, *love* itches my sore hands
reminds me of the days,
alone that, I spent.
The memories of you, the flickers of heartache,
my love tainted hands and the sorrows you gave.
My appetite grew,
I cook a lot these days
and sometimes end up plating two plates,
two glasses of water
one for you, one for me
I keep waiting for you so aimlessly
no, you never come
nor did you call
and now the plant in my garden
bores fruits for us all.
Two seasons have passed
and so has the time for you,
I just finished writing the letter,
the letter that, I'll never send you.

Today, I'm letting you go
letting you off, from every fragment of my being,
setting free all the locked up memories
as, I throw away the key.
I'm making room for love
while, I set you free
without longing
along with the cold breeze.
You've been in my heart for long
longer that, I've ever been
and it's time, I let you go
and let someone else in.
You broke the walls inside
stole me from all my love
but it's time, I take out my hidden stash
and give someone else a chance.

Love shows up at my door
and, I ask “where have you been?”
“that’s a long story” he says,
now where do, I begin.
I was here last June,
when you sealed shut the door,
when you believed, I’ll never have it
I was there, standing at your door.
I was here last fall
when, you fell for him, I watched
I knew he would break your heart
but for your smile,
I was willing to take the chance.
I was here when you cried,
when you made chocolate covered strawberries
and ate every last bite,

I was there, I watched
I waited for the time to be finally right.
I saw you stand in front of the mirror
and hate everything you wore,
if you ask me, for the clothes to feel your skin
was their greatest honor.
To me you were always perfect,
never too much nor too less
and when he broke your heart,
something in me felt the wreck
and I had to watch, ‘cos the timing wasn’t right
but it took everything in me
not to run after you just to hold you tight.
To be honest, I was always there
I never left you alone,
in fact you were too full of me
how could you not have known?

Writing this was my dream
and for anyone who got this far in reading it,
You helped me live it.
Thank you!!

Thank you to my muse, you know who you are ;)
You helped inspire the book by being your utterly perfect self and
the grief that followed in picturing a life without you.

Thank you to Srishti, Abhey and all my friends who read every
single thought that, I planted onto the paper and showed me an
unwavering amount of support.
I couldn't have done it without you all.
also, a special thank you to my friend Shreya for hand drawing
most of these beautiful illustrations. You all can find her as
@eterna1_chaos on Instagram.

and

Thank you to my parents,
this is where, I fall short on words so,
here's a little something for you-

For my Mum,

I've heard people say that one reincarnates
and gets a new life just as good as their deeds were in the last,
but, I can't possibly imagine
what in the world could, I have possibly done that,
I got you as my mum,
someone who gave birth to me,
someone who loved every single part of me
even long before it was formed.
I can't possibly imagine
what did, I do
that I got to have you, love you
and know how wonderful of a person you are.
I don't think, I could ever tell you enough
about how much, I love you,
but whenever something happens,
you're the only person, I want to run to.
You make it easier for me to breathe
and make me stronger even when, I turned weak.
You're a poem,
I can never write enough verses to
'cos getting the privilege to call you my mum
makes me feel the way, no happiness in the world could do.

For my Dad,

You've been the best dad ever
and, I won't lie and say,
we've been perfect,
'cos when it comes to
being in a room alone with you,
I find trouble thinking of what to say.
It's like, I want to keep talking
and laughing with you
but words come out easier on paper
you know,
I've always been this way.
Lately, I hug you
every time you come home
or, I go out- I hug you
as if, I'm screaming 'I love you' out loud,
as, I wrap my arms around you,
you hug me back tighter-
as if it's an 'I love you too'.

Thank you!

You can find me on

Instagram as- @manyawritesss

YouTube as- @manyawritess

Tik Tok as- @manyawrites